# Show us Your Fire

# Show us Your Fire

## JOY DONNELL

**SUPERJOY**
media

Set in 8/10/12 point Cardo

ISBN 978-1-7341243-4-7 (paperback)
ISBN 978-1-7341243-5-4 (hardcover)
ISBN 978-1-7341243-5-4 (audiobook)

Library of Congress Control Number: 2023900601

Donnell, Joy
    Show Us Your Fire / Joy Donnell

First printing edition 2023

*This book is dedicated to*
AMIRA
BILY
DRU
JASMINE
JULIA
PAFF
*and*
PRIYANKA

*The author would like to thank*
JOY R. BOSTIC
*for her excited work about African American female
mysticism, which helped the lineage of the work be
realized.*

ETHOS DELEON
*for their viral post about decolonizing spirituality and
personal development.*

NICOLE HAGGARD
*for her groundbreaking research about the lasting impact of
Hollywood's hidden history of racism and sexual racism on
screen, which largely influenced this collection.*

*and*
DRISANA (DRU) McDANIEL
*for her tireless work on radical self-integration.*

*It's not your job to dismantle the systems*
*that give you less than you deserve,*
*but you can resist them*
*by affirming your own worth.*
— Lola Bakare

# CONTENTS

✳

**curiosity requires**
a gentle approach
a softening
to all things possible
even if inexplicable;
an unlearning of that
unyielding harshness
with which
you've been taught
to step towards everything,
including yourself.

suddenly,
you turn inward
to a mirror that helps
you face yourself
with reverence
instead of ridicule.

✳

**I wake remembering** my place in a lineage that made a way out of no way. So I continue to make space for the possible within the impossible, for the figuring out of absurdity, for the pieces of me so impractical, they defy any and all doubt that I am guiding myself home.

✳

**if you want fear**
**to dissipate**,
never doubt your magic.
if you want your gifts
to grow,
realize
peace of mind
as the soil
for abundance.
exhaustion plays tricks
with your talents.
it makes you forget
your energy is your power.
your defiance
in the face of injustice
is your discernment.
Let your senses rest.
Let your emotions rest.
This, too, is productivity.
Take the space needed
to build a wonder palace
for your solace.

3

# TENDER

Tenderly.
How I recline
into my needs.
How I teleport
from high alert
into priceless awareness.

Certainly,
tension always grabs
our attention.
But,
comfort sharpens focus.

Decolonization begins
with enjoyment of teeny,
tiny things:
Lilies. Laughter. Long naps.
Being
versus doing.
Noticing
liminal space between.

For it is at edges —
these seams —
where what I know deeply
to be true
meets the lies
I have been told.

Here it is.
My body is my earthly home.
Remarkably, my life is my own.
Nothing alive is alien to me.

Interconnection.
Undeniable.

Within edges,
my invitation to all things.

Along seams
I start to understand
how seamless I am.
How I have spirit
and somehow I am spirit.

How I have nature
and somehow I am nature.

At this threshold,
such light.
such shadow.
Prayers of ancestors
I've never known
pushing everything to the center.

My mission
staring my marauders down.

All those pirates, exposed,
having nowhere to hide.

# A GENERATIVE QUESTION PROPELS ME

how might I
recognize myself
as medicine
instead of messiness?

✳

**Liberation**
cannot be
centered
without joy
as its nucleus.

＊

**There is also sacred disruption**. We find it within nature, so naturally within our lived experience. Wisdom has named the energy over and over. It characterizes deities who aren't to be trifled with once in motion. The ferocious compassion of Kali Ma, obliterator of illusion and corrector of injustice. It is the volcanic way that Pele destroys as she creates.

For us, it accompanies curiosity. The questions that arise when we meet unpleasantness and inhumanity. It is the inquiry we do when we notice we feel unaligned and misnamed.

Curiosity is a spiritual technology. Toddlers have it as a trait. Adults can nourish it as skill. It is encoded within our spirit so that we can activate growth at whim, willfully. It is not meant to be fleeting phenomena when it can crack you open and form new geography in the ocean of your energy.

✳

**well, imperial plunder** looted my heirloom looking glass and handed me a warped lens. Garbage. I've had to trash it.

Almost every idea on how to be human, respectable, worthy — shaped by a eugenicist.

Someone that decided they knew precisely who needed to be celebrated and who must be culled.

People who measured human skulls to access the value of a human life.

The broken lens disregards the poetry of the body, the spectrum of ability, the effervescence of ancestry, the alchemical arts of self compassion.

It claims the body has no meaning except as a tool for performance and productivity.

It claims I should be put to work[1] [2] [3] and worked to death. I can find rest in the afterlife.

It provides only the dialects of colonizing and conquering as innerspeak: Mind over body. Control my emotions. I against I. My inner saboteur. Me as my own worst enemy.

*I can't acquire the definition*
*of myself from how*
*unhealthy people and systems*
*want to define me.*

---

1   I heard about a clipping from 1918.
    Greenville, SC in an uproar. Black women acting uppity, dare I say leisurely. Refusing work. And without Black women the White-bodied women had no one to cook or be a laundress, or help them raise their kids.
2   Of course, these Black women had their own families needful of their energy.
3   Still, Greenville screamed, "Loafs! Lazy!" and *The Greenville News* printed, "Negro Women To Be Put To Work". Any Black woman who refused and could not show papers proving she was employed, would be jailed or heavily fined. Per city ordinance.

＊

**Grace is an energy.**
It flows to
and through you.
It is lightning
seeking the tree.
It is the fire
sleeping
within the wood
*before the strike.*

# QUALIA

The more convinced I am of my wholeness, the less I want to divide myself. The less I am to wage war with my authenticity, with my growth, with my future self.
Instead, I wonder.

I explore being in partnership with my body, my sanctuary. I want to give it my companionship. Move en tandem with this bridge as it pulls my dreams into my hands.

I welcome this container as a sage, protector, healer, collaborator, co-conspirator, confidante that never lies to me, even while ignored.

*The gut*
*rumbling*
*with intuition.*

*My heart*
*stretching towards*
*what thrills me.*

*My nerves tingling*
*as I uncover*
*cosmic breadcrumbs*
*leading to my future.*

*My jaw clenching*
*from biting my tongue*
*during structural terror.*

The body provides safe haven for our rich interiority.
An archive housing the archivist.
Flesh offering the vast eternal a location,
coordinates within the now.

Once your nervous system understands what brings you calm and freedom, it becomes difficult for it to accept their prolonged absence. Like a divining rod, sense memory tells you where to dig.

Your passion, courage, defiance.
Equal part signals and spells.
All guidance to your mystical liberating space calling from within.

✳

You've been in survival mode
because there is structural violence.

You've been in psychospiritual distress
because you have been encouraged
to normalize your nervous system to
less than you deserve.

When thriving isn't a fluent language in our
environments, most will be shown ways of
coping masquerading as actual healing.

We repeat as we are shown,
not as we are told.

# WHAT WE KEEP

my love
my sweetest being
has the softness within you
been invaded?
has the intruder's invective
planted its flag?
stripped you bare
then called you beast?
misnamed your gods as myths?
shaved your hair
within which you had
hidden heirloom seeds?
co opted your ancestral science
only to pronounce you primitive?
sacrificed your body as labor
but declared you lacking?
impregnated your
vivacious truth
with soulless monotony?

there was a time before this
if you dare to remember
when you knew your prophecy
inside and out
yes, you still know it
and this is why
you think you languish
my dearest defiant one
this is not suffering,
it is deep knowing
this is not frustration,
it is recollection
these are not your tears,
this is rain replenishing
the parched earth.

come to the innerspace
where you are held
without self-rejection
it doesn't matter if
you forgot for a moment
how to adore it

your beauty never left you
like a beloved
tattered teddy bear
you once embraced
each night while dreaming
but had to abandon
in order to toughen
into this world
it simply waits
for you to once again
regard yourself
its steward.

# HOME REMEDIES

the medicine for boredom is imagination.
the medicine for frustration is creating.
the medicine for anxiety is gratitude.
the medicine for rejection is resilience.
the medicine for shame is self compassion.
the medicine for self doubt is self awareness.

# WHY DO YOU RUN FROM YOURSELF?

There is something
about holding
your beauty
and
your horror
in the same bittersweet embrace
that will make a believer
out of you… you're obligated
to protect your energy.

Suddenly,
there will be no need
to fetishize struggle
you won't even
feel like running
since this
tender magic we call your body
is weary
since the
only place to go
is deeper

since the
ancient defiance
within you
has been patient
for your homecoming.

✳

**Bloom as needed.**
And when fragrant petals
have to fall away
when your energy must recirculate
so that new growth may form,
welcome the pause.
Your need for
replenishment is also natural.
You require what you require
without apology.

## TO BEGIN AGAIN, YOU BURN

*Are you my ancestor?*
I ask this flame
(Not with words).
Energy talks to energy...

the universe speaks to
us in a daring dialect,
an esperanto of grit and grace.
It whispers through
the phoenix, "burn away
everything no longer
needed, my sweetness,
and rise again
as your own fire."

## A WORLD ALIVE.

Trickery
can always be undone.
Any veil can be unveiled
so once you call forth the courage
to remember you are worthy
of your own compassion
you'll find yourself touching the rock
and without hesitation it touches you back
turtledoves become fortunate omens
their excrement spiraled
on your balcony ledge: a cosmic blessing;
auspicious
the night blooming jasmine
map shimmering scent passageways
to that threshold beyond surrender itself.
Look around.
You are in a world alive.

## THE LOVER

Empathy begins
with attentiveness.
As does creativity.
Even romance.

I am having an epic love affair with my
nervous system, my heart, solar plexus, each
chakra, the populations existing within me.
Romance isn't overtures and grand gestures.
What makes it unmistakable is awareness,
noticing a need easily missed. How my jaw
unclenches. When my shoulders drop. Places
and people that put knots in my stomach.
Spaces that nourish calm.

I listen with my breath. Flow is my north star.

I have only to be a giver to myself of what I
need. Be observant, a most devoted lover. Use
my comfort as a portal to remembering what I
love and want to create with my life force.

Self-kindness is wild and seeding, growing like kudzu over ever false narrative taking up real estate in my mind.

It becomes habitual, thinking and feeling my way into radical self love. Readily, I see that I am portal within a portal. I seek the places of connection. They feel like a secret formula, and, alchemical path.

I let what sweetly whispers from the natural world draw me closer. Sniff jasmine. Eye sparrows. Drift in the distant vistas enticing my adventurous spirit through coherence and mystery. Dip my body in the instruments of sweetwaters and saltwaters. Feel the eternal grounded in nowness.

I know what calls me. Within, we know what beckons to us, uniquely.

Integration, this beloved confidante of the eternal beauty stretching within me.

## GALAXY

We are taught to fix our eyes to outer space
hoping for signs of life, some inkling that we
are not alone, yet we move through the world
as a galaxy teeming with life. Gut bacteria
radiating good vibes in our brain,
mitochondria holding the memories of
matrilineal trauma. Microscopic mutualism
living in flow with us, stressing with our
stress, thriving with our thriving. We have
never been alone.

✳

the audacity
of romantic living
requests of you
an allowing
a new vocabulary
to birth itself within
you
this is the overture
a body of ideas
whispering from
cell to cell
like sweet nothings
between lovers.

**Focus only on what you want.**
Feel into it.
Use the energy of your ancestral courage,
what you're made of, to fuel your vision.
Remember that you are why the ancestors did
all those rituals. They persevered so you can
become.

Within this deep knowing, be endless.

# GENERATIVE QUESTION NO. 2

where might I
reclaim my birthright
to benevolent community?

*

I've met enough horror to close myself off, and be justified, yet I move through this world with both hands open, ready to give and receive, refusing bitterness, rebuking a deadening, allowing this flame to rise from my unshakeable palm.

✳

**You are a future ancestor.** The richness flowing through you will be called upon when folks need to remember: they don't have to wait for permission because they are the change. They don't have to wait for healing. They are the restoration.

**Every part of me loves me**, even the traumatized parts. Even my fears speak up out of love and will be proud of me when I ignore them. No part of me is out to get me. Every corner of my being is rooting for me. My past, present, and future selves all want me to be and become.

# RESTORATIVE NARRATIVES

My courage crafts a restorative narrative, one serving compassion and flow. One that loves the poetry of my body. One that doesn't need rugged individualism or toxic collectivity. Something embodying the expansive truth between. One that realizes extremes are not real choices. That refuses to be pushed from one far side to another, being herded disguised as liberation. Authentic. A story that holds and rocks me at its bosom, humming, healing, disrupting this world with my fullness.

✳

Our higher goal is always equitable self-determination. When equity isn't being offered, many will accept a compromised sense of belonging in hopes at having a shot at being safe. We know we need community in order to survive. Belonging is our birthright.

Too many of us find ourselves in spaces we thought were welcoming us in, only, to discover we were lured. Worse still, segregated. Funneled into corners of fear. Intended to become easy prey. The suburb you choose and the ghetto you don't. The cult you join or the internment camp you're shipped to... its amazing how desperation can concentrate.

When the prey learn the ways of the terror, it becomes clear, predators are rigid. They hope the trauma they inflict will make you rigid: freeze, flight, fight, fawn; pick only one and lack fluidity.

Homogeneity helps hegemonic violence pin a target down. That's why it hopes you will check a box. It wants you finite and stuck, so it knows exactly where to find you.

communal horror
always demands
communal healing.
individual remedies
alone
are insufficient.

# REFRAME

the real culprit is the hand that crams the crabs into the bucket. forces them into trauma. concentrates agony. buckets are neither indifferent nor intentioned. buckets don't desire or map methodology to extract and consume. a bucket is not an eater. it is a tool of separation repurposed into contained terror; the set and setting of communal horror. it is invaluable to know and name the unnatural elements that elicit the natural trauma response. conditions are revealed by who gets nourished and who is expected to languish in misery.

✳

**A balanced throat chakra** isn't just about compassionately and fearlessly speaking truth to power. It's also about deep listening and holding sacred social space for what others need to convey, for the work that needs to be done. It's also about creating a container.

✳

**This era is moving** away from
transactional to relational,
from hierarchies to networks,
from speed to slowing down,
from volume to value,
from solo destiny
to shared destiny.

Now
let us heal within community.

✳

Once you lean into **the calling**,
You'll realize why it
Didn't happen before now.
You'll understand that
The change was waiting for you.

# GENERATIVE QUESTION NO. 3

where might I cultivate
a space that nourishes
my spark of defiance?

✳

**I study
the art of ease**
as a form of faith.
Deep belly breaths
as the fuel of devotion.
Compassion is
an action verb.

✳

**In creating art every day,**
it will become clear that
you yourself are art:
a masterpiece unfolding.
And when you tell
the tale of your awakening,
it will become unclear
if you are a storyteller
or a mystic.
Because you are both.

## INNER SPEAK

Every strong woman you know was once in bed, curled into a fetal position, wailing, desperate, longing for her mama (any kind of mothering), convinced she was broken, fearful she would never be made whole, yet, a sweet voice deep inside, older than pride or doubt or our yellow sun, lifted her up, helped her wipe her tears and keep holding on to herself.

## VISIONARY

Your vision roots itself in an unwavering
loyalty to gratitude when you know your
heart is capable of worldbuilding, that you
have always been a universe moving within a
universe, that you simply speaking your
dreams aloud releases them, cosmically, across
distance and time
just as thermals rising from the earth updraft
the dandelion so its seeds can take flight.

## 5 FORMS OF DISTRACTION FROM YOUR POWER

1 Staying in the wrong place because you're scared to leave.
2 Trying to prove yourself to people who don't respect your humanity.
3 Giving all your energy to others because you're secretly convinced that you're not enough.
4 Over-committing so that you never have time to focus on yourself, your passions, your goals or projects.
5 Trying to expand the minds of people who don't desire growth.

# THE EVIDENCE OF MAGIC

One day I realized
I can journey into
the deepest
despair in my mind
and return with
something beautiful.

That's my proof.
I am transformative.
I am whole
and healing wondrously.
I will remain
fabulous and defiant.

Even my revolt
is a beginning.

## CHOICES

We can always count on collective amnesia. Betrayal, once seen, prefers to flaunt itself in every corner of every experience you once believed was genuine and good. *And who wants that waving in your face? Most would rather look away and pretend.* Getting conned makes you question if everything has been a lie. If you have been scammed. If you are in a world lousy with pirates. A culture of domination cannot thrive without populations forgetting. Of course, you remember all the way down to your cells. The past is living its future.

Nonetheless, you do not have to be the keeper of the flame, the historian of hidden history, the conjurer of lost arts. Of course, there is no ignoring what is still happening. There is no misidentifying what has simply changed its avatar or undergone a massive rebranding.

Regardless it isn't your duty to remember. Recollection is your right. If you choose it. Only if you choose it.

We give language to what we reclaim as we gather within this space borderless and bonded by the modalities of lightworkers, lucid dreamers, mystics and moon readers, high priestesses and healers, keepers of earthseeds and starseeds, poets of interbeauty, guardians of sweetwaters and water benders, firetalkers, the othermothers of oneness and collective liberation.

What was once sequestered in solitude is now linked through solidarity, working in cahoots, aligned in the edict of Pachamama to create an earth common home for the living.

We tell a new story for a new earth, a replenishment that knows we are the soil and seeds, the gardeners and the bumper crop.

✳

**In your voice**
you will find
a sword beside a garden.
Wield
whichever weapon
you need.

✳

**Undoubtedly**, some of us have to be the ones to say it aloud. We have to call out the trauma, betrayal, damage inflicted and endured even though it will disrupt everything. It will blow up the structure of pain and denial that everyone has learned to depend on. Some of us have to be the ones to say, "Enough." Say it so smoothly that it transmutes into a prayer.

**Equity is not a finite resource.**
Especially when we understand it
as love. Adaptable, it can stretch and squeeze
into any space, mold itself to the specificity of
one as well as masses. It can fill a spirit and
swaddle a weary soul. Championing equity is
a centering of love.

**Some of us have family members** deeply vested in the lineage of trauma. Their power and status within the family is tethered to it. So, while they love you, they'll hurt, attack, and sabotage any of your work to heal the generational trauma because that healing will disrupt their influence.

## ALLOWING

Be open.
Wow yourself.
You know you
deserve a better story
than what you have
been offered.
Let this whole world
become
your spellbook.

## ORIGIN OF PEARLS

A mollusk can
turn a parasite into a pearl.
Perhaps you learned
these gems begin as
grains of sand.
They aren't tiny irritants,
but former would-be invaders.
Sand, after all, involves
an oyster's natural state of being.
Intruders are a different story,
getting encased in milky magic
until unrecognizable.
Instinct, this inner wisdom
perfected over
millions of years until harnessed
as a superpower
capable of turning a marauder
into a daughter of the moon.
And what will you make
of what aims to invade your mind?
How will you uphold your sanctuary?

✳

**If I am a myth,**
who should be the storyteller?
If I am a dream,
who gets to be the dreamer?

What we habitually believe
about the quality
of the unfolding moment
is what uncovers
the opportunity presenting itself.

Recognize that the space between
where you are and where you wish to be
is also sacred.

✳

Having a strategy or **ambition is still faith**. The natural world has strategies all the time. Flowers don't just expect to propagate through osmosis or manifesting. They release pollen. They involve bees. They evoke hope. Strategically. Call it grand design. Or nature. Pollination is planning future-forward. I see evidence of a conscious world; all consciousness must harmonize strategy (action/intention) with surrender (trust/faith).

# TIME TRAVELER

I came to this world to meet myself.
To discover what is possible with this energy.
To make tangible what was once intangible.
To make real what others can't even envision.
To keep healing myself as I become a harvest manifesting.
To be a change agent, remembering the dreams of microbes frozen on asteroids hurdling through deep space, longing for a planetary oasis to call home.

✳

Perhaps you have always felt a bit **set apart** from this world. Consider that you didn't come here to harmonize with your environment's bs. Be careful what you blend in with. Your energy changes a space. If you feel the urge to be a bright color, don't fight it. Remain steadfast in self regard when the surroundings seek to dim you.

You arrive as a cosmic seed to grow something new. Your presence is more necessary than your perfection. Remain too vast and vibrant. Your time and energy is not meant to be speedily and violently consumed.

## UNIFIER

Yes, know the rules
so you can break them
like an artist.
Also know
who made the rules
so you can break them
as an abolitionist.
Know
who the rules benefit
so you can break them
like a strategist.
Know
who the rules divide
and conquer so you can
break them
as a unifier.

# MEET ME RIGHT HERE

When you are weary,
wary, fearing you will be forever frenzied;
Pause. Sit with me.
Together we will remember
what we stand for.
We will call upon Rosa,
one of many who came before us
to model how to remain seated
who shut down a whole system
by staying put
reclaiming rest.

When you feel separated,
set apart, without tribe,
trapped and tricked;
Pause. Grab my hand.
Hold on to your lineage,
every visionary has ancestry
someone before who in the
midst of chaos journeyed inward
to a sovereign space
where we've always known
we have every right to be free.

*It is said that Harriet*
*had sleeping spells.*
*She would project into realms*
*from which no one could stir her,*
*then, awake with the exact plan*
*for evasion*
*and we already know she was never caught.*

When you are exhausted,
stretched so thin,
you almost respond
to those who misname you;
Pause. Talk to me.
Tell me your secret name.
Is it Love? Is it Life? Wholeness?
I will state it with the full biometric field of
my heart, the oldest language of the living,
how the tree speaks to the tree.

*Sojourner said that Spirit whispered to her to*
*change her name from Isabella.*
*So she released that chained identity.*
*We now know her by what she chose, not what*
*was foisted.*

63

Pause. Relax. Be at ease so we can behold one another. In community. Together, as we become an edgeless mirror.

## REAL PEACE REQUIRES COLLISION

We are the beneficiaries
of so much collision
gifting us all we know
to be healing
even the holy waters
we journey to for rebirth
arrived
around 3.8 billion years ago
in a comet crashing to earth
delivering this
elemental force,
changing the world,
giving us what are now
reflective horizons
we gaze into
for breath-filled tranquility.
Behold, the peace born
from forces colliding.

✳

**In the morning**, the first thing
I reach for is the sunlight,
this dawning within
and outside myself.

I want moments
as clean as quartz.
Without distraction.
Nothing to qualify.
Or quantify.
No pushing.
Only attraction drawing
me closer to what is
cellular and worthy
of loving notice.

**I prefer**
to keep
some parts
of myself
unruly.

✳

**I have arrived** to transgress and cross boundaries that never should have been.
To uproot and root out.
Cosmic Mama guides me with one hand, the other hand steady on her hip, fed up with foolishness. "Go on, baby," she tells my soul. "Do what you came here to do."

✳

**I went looking**
for all the awe
in the universe.
Naturally,
I've discovered
I am made of it.

## Support *Show Us Your Fire*

I hope this book serves you well. If you think more people should read it, here are ways you can support:

1. **Recommend it** to others.
2. **Leave a review** on GoodReads, Amazon, or wherever you got your copy.
3. **Share and talk about it** on social media, post pictures, and use #showusyourfire.
4. **Gift a copy** of the book to friends, family, mentees, mentors, and colleagues.
5. **Request it at your local library** or college/university library. If several people ask a library for a title, they will order copies to shelve.
6. **Suggest it to book clubs,** reading groups, and event gift bags.
7. **Suggest Joy as a speaker** at your school, social and professional organizations, panels and keynotes.
8. **Host a book reading, dinner, or party**. If you are part of a book club or dinner group that meets virtually and/or in-person, please consider inviting Joy to be a special guest.

# **About** *Show Us Your Fire*

*Show Us Your Fire* is a collection of poetry and prose about radical self-love. It explores the freedom in owning your birthright to self-compassion and a full life. Joy Donnell examines the distractions, chaos, and exhaustion that make us feel fragmented within ourselves. Through meditations, memory, instinct, and intuition, this mystical journey looks at how to integrate our whole selves into our own lives.

This is an invitation to be. Take up space. Declare your needs without apology.

Do not blend in with what is unaligned.
Your fullness is meant to be disruptive.

Together, we will create a sacred container of beloved community.
Here, hustle and grind gives way to ease and flow.
Simply come home to yourself.

# About *Joy Donnell*

Joy Donnell is a producer and writer focused on the psychospiritual power of storytelling. Her work has been featured in *W*, *HuffPost*, and *Buzzfeed*. She is cofounder of **CIME**, The Center for Intersectional Media and Entertainment, which researches how stories make us feel and the tools needed to tell restorative narratives.

## STAY CONNECTED

Twitter, LinkedIn, Instagram @doitinpublic

## ALSO BY JOY DONNELL

### *Beyond Brand*

You're human. You deserve to be more than a brand. *Beyond Brand* is a personal development book that dives into personal legacy. It expands the ideas of your power, inner joy and media outreach to build a culture you can live in real-time as well as leave behind. Through stories, self examination, best practices and strategy, Donnell breaks down how to keep what you create aligned with who you are becoming. Live your legacy.

Made in the USA
Las Vegas, NV
15 March 2023

69159690R00052